DATE DUE

Careers without College

Tractor-Trailer-Truck Driver

by Susan Clinton

Content Consultant:
James H. Lewis
Office of Public Affairs
American Trucking Association

CAPSTONE BOOKS
an imprint of Capstone Press
Mankato, Minnesota

Capstone Books are published by Capstone Press
151 Good Counsel Drive, P.O. Box 669, Mankato, Minnesota 56002
http://www.capstone-press.com

Library of Congress Cataloging-in-Publication Data
Clinton, Susan.
    Tractor-trailer-truck driver/by Susan Clinton.
      p. cm.--(Careers without college)
    Includes bibliographical references (p. 45) and index.
    Summary: Outlines the educational requirements, duties,
salary, employment outlook, and possible future positions of
tractor-trailer-truck drivers.
    ISBN 1-56065-710-3
    1. Truck driving--Vocational guidance--Juvenile literature.
[1. Truck driving--Vocational guidance. 2. Vocational guidance.]
I. Title. II. Series: Careers without college (Mankato, Minn.)
TL230.3.C55 1998
388.3'24'024--DC21

                                  97-35225
                                     CIP
                                     AC

Photo Credits:
California Trucking Association, 9
Betty Crowell, 28
Peter S. Ford, cover, 44;
International Stock/Mark Bolster, 6; Bob Firth, 25; Andre Jenny, 43; Dario
    Perla, 11; Westerman, 4
Leslie O'Shaughnessy, 31, 38
Unicorn Stock Photos/Chromosohm/Sohm, 14, 37; Nancy Ferguson, 22;
    A. Ramey, 27; Ted Rose, 34; H. Schmeiser, 20; Joe Sohm, 32
Valan Photos/Jean Bruneau, 12; Joyce Photographics, 17; J.E. Stevenson, 41

Table of Contents

Fast Facts

Career Title _____ Tractor-trailer-truck driver

Minimum Educational Requirement _____ High school diploma

Certification Requirement _____ Federal license requirements

U.S. Salary Range _____ $15,000 to $50,000

Canadian Salary Range _____ $12,700 to $49,300 (Canadian dollars)

U.S. Job Outlook _____ Faster than the average

Canadian Job Outlook _____ Faster than the average

DOT Cluster _____ Miscellaneous occupations
(Dictionary of Occupational Titles)

DOT Number _____ 904.383-010

GOE Number _____ 05.08.01
(Guide for Occupational Exploration)

NOC _____ 7411
(National Occupational Classification—Canada)

Chapter 1

Job Responsibilities

Tractor-trailer-truck drivers move goods and products from one place to another. Sometimes truck drivers move parts from one factory to another. Other times truck drivers carry finished products from factories to warehouses or stores. Tractor-trailer-truck drivers carry many of the goods people use every day.

Tractor-trailer-truck drivers carry many of the goods people use every day.

Duties

Truck drivers deliver food to grocery stores. They deliver fuel to gas stations. People depend on trucks to carry their belongings when they move to new homes.

Tractor-trailer-truck drivers move packages from city to city. Trucks also carry mail. Manufacturers, farmers, and retailers depend on tractor-trailer-truck drivers to deliver products.

Types of Employment

Most tractor-trailer-truck drivers work for trucking companies. Trucking companies supply trucks. Company mechanics take care of and fix the trucks. Other employees assign each driver's route and schedule. A route is the plan a driver follows while making deliveries. A schedule is a preset timetable.

Most tractor-trailer-truck drivers work for trucking companies.

CON-WAY
INTERMODAL

MC 189836
GW 80000

About one out of every 10 tractor-trailer-truck drivers is self-employed. This means they do not work for just one company. They haul goods for many companies. But they work for themselves.

Some tractor-trailer-truck drivers own their own trucks. These drivers are owner-operators. Owner-operators set their own routes. They choose the loads they carry. Owner-operators also have to pay for their own truck repairs. They must compete for business with big companies.

Owner-operators choose the goods they carry.

Chapter 2

What the Job Is Like

Some tractor-trailer-truck drivers make many stops in one city every day. Other drivers may be away from home for weeks at a time. Both types of drivers haul goods from one place to another.

Local Drivers

Tractor-trailer-truck drivers who drive in one city every day are local drivers. Many local drivers deliver food to stores. Some local drivers carry

Some local drivers carry gas from fuel plants to gas stations.

gas from fuel plants to gas stations. Local drivers often work the same routes each week. They are rarely away from home overnight.

Local drivers get to know their customers. Sometimes local drivers help sell their companies' products to store owners. Local drivers pick up or drop off part of their load at each stop. They do a lot of lifting.

Local drivers usually work in cities. Driving these routes can be hard. Traffic may be heavy. Turning a big truck onto narrow streets and alleys can be a challenge. Many local tractor-trailer-truck drivers start working early in the morning. This helps them avoid heavy traffic.

Some days, driving local routes takes longer than eight hours. But local drivers can go home every night. Not all tractor-trailer-truck drivers can do that.

Local drivers pick up or drop off part of their loads at each stop.

Some tractors pull two or three big trailers.

Long-Haul Driving

Some tractor-trailer-truck drivers travel between cities and states. Their routes may cover thousands of miles. These drivers are long-haul drivers. Another name for long-haul drivers is

over-the-road drivers. Some over-the-road drivers
use their tractors to pull two or three big trailers.
A tractor is the front part of a truck where the
driver sits. The tractor contains the engine of the

truck. The part of the vehicle that carries the goods is called the trailer.

Some over-the-road drivers have routes between cities. They can drive, unload, and drive back in one day. These routes are called turnarounds.

Many long-haul drivers drive on trips that take a week or longer. Two drivers may travel together on long trips. These drivers are sleeper teams. Drivers in sleeper teams take turns. One driver sleeps in the back of the cab. The cab is the passenger part of the tractor. The other driver drives the truck. Sleeper teams do not have to stop as often for rest. They can make trips faster than single drivers.

Long-haul drivers spend much of their time away from home. Long-haul driving can be lonely. But drivers have many opportunities to meet people while they are on the road.

Long-haul driving can be lonely.

Chapter 3

Training

All tractor-trailer-truck drivers must have a state driver's license. Drivers must also have good driving records. Employers want to hire safe drivers. Drivers who are reckless or careless will have a hard time finding jobs. Trucks and their contents are valuable. Employers want drivers to take good care of company trucks.

State License

A state license only allows drivers to operate small, light trucks. Drivers usually have to be at least 21

Employers want drivers to take good care of company trucks.

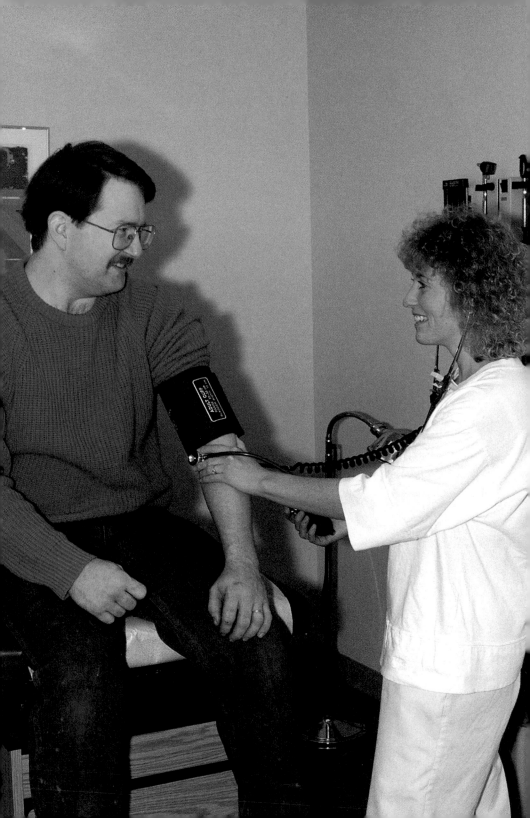

years old to drive tractor-trailer trucks. Only drivers who are at least 21 years old can drive interstate routes. Interstate means across state lines. Most long-haul trucking companies want drivers who are 25 years old or older.

Interstate drivers must pass a written test on safety rules. They must also pass a medical examination. Doctors check them for good hearing and good vision. Drivers must be in good health to perform their jobs.

Commercial Driver's License (CDL)

Most tractor-trailer-truck drivers need a commercial driver's license (CDL). Truck drivers must have CDLs to drive heavy trucks. They need CDLs to drive tractor-trailer trucks.

To get CDLs, drivers must pass a written test and a driving test. The written test covers traffic laws and rules of safe driving. Drivers must know how to drive in snow. They must also know how to steer out of skids. This means they must know how to stop trailers from sliding off the road. Truck

Tractor-trailer-truck drivers must be in good health.

drivers also need to know what to do if an accident happens.

Laws limit the amount of weight trucks can carry. Drivers must know weight limits for their trucks. Laws also prevent drivers from driving tractor-trailer trucks on certain roads. Drivers must understand laws that apply to truck driving.

The CDL driving test shows how well drivers can handle big trucks. Drivers must be able to turn in tight corners. They must show that they can back trucks up to loading docks. They must be able to link trailers to tractors in no more than 10 minutes.

It is hard for some people to practice driving. Most people do not own trucks. Some trucking companies train their new drivers. Most people learn to drive big trucks by attending truck driving schools.

Truck Driving Schools

Truck driving schools prepare drivers to pass CDL tests. Instructors teach students how to drive

The driving test shows how well drivers can handle big trucks.

different kinds of trucks. These schools let students practice in different kinds of trucks.

Drivers learn about safety. They learn about the trucks they drive and how the trucks work. Students learn safety rules such as how to brake. They learn not to drive too fast or follow other automobiles too closely. Drivers also learn to stop driving when they feel tired. Tired drivers can cause accidents.

Good programs offer about 147 hours of instruction. The Professional Truck Driver Institute of America certifies truck driving schools that meet certain standards. Certify means to officially approve.

Truck driving schools charge money for their courses. The amount varies from school to school. The cost of training can range from $2,300 to $5,000. Many schools help students apply for jobs after they finish the courses. But schools do not promise to find jobs for students.

Most people learn to drive big trucks by attending truck driving schools.

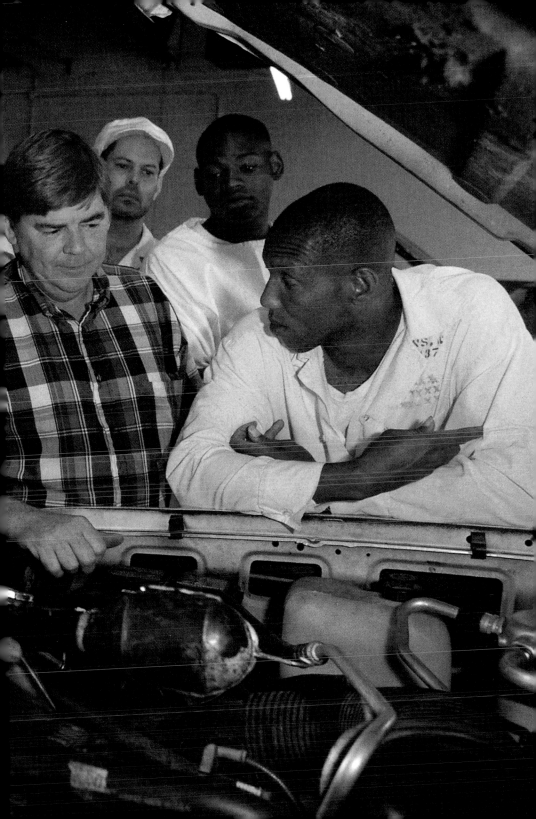

Drivers need endorsements to drive tankers.

Additional Training

Drivers can receive extra training to earn endorsements on their CDLs. An endorsement is proof of additional driving abilities. Each

endorsement qualifies drivers for special kinds of
driving. Truck drivers need endorsements to drive
doubles. A double is a tractor that pulls two

trailers. Drivers also need endorsements to drive tankers. A tanker is a truck that carries liquids.

Drivers carrying hazardous materials must have endorsements. Hazardous materials are chemicals that could hurt people or make them sick. These materials could spill or catch on fire in an accident. Drivers must know how to haul these materials safely.

Useful Subjects to Study

People who want to be truck drivers should study math. Drivers keep track of the weight of their trucks. They keep daily logs of the miles they drive. Drivers record the amount of goods they pick up and deliver. They keep track of customers' orders.

Knowing about geography is also useful. Geography is the study of the earth. Truck drivers must be skilled at reading maps. They must be aware of weather and road conditions.

Long-haul drivers check their trucks for safety before every trip. They check the brakes, the

Tractor-trailer-truck drivers must understand how trucks work.

engine, the steering, and other systems. They must understand how trucks work.

Sometimes trucks have problems. Drivers may need to make engine repairs. They may have to change tires or adjust the brakes. They may have to jump-start trucks that have dead batteries. Drivers can learn how to handle these problems by taking courses in auto mechanics.

Finding Jobs

Drivers under 21 years old may have a hard time finding truck driving jobs. Some drivers start as helpers for local drivers. Other truck drivers get started by serving in the Armed Forces. Military driving experience can help people get truck driving jobs.

Some young people work on the loading docks at trucking companies. They load trucks for drivers. They may drive forklifts to stack heavy goods. Workers learn where drivers go and how companies keep records. Employers sometimes promote qualified workers to truck driver positions.

Some people work on the loading docks at trucking companies.

STRAUSS VEAL
FEEDS, INC.
NORTH MANCHESTER, IN
WATERTOWN, WI

Chapter 4

Salary and Job Outlook

Some local tractor-trailer-truck drivers receive hourly pay. They can earn from $9 to $15 per hour. Truck drivers who work more than 40 hours per week earn overtime pay. Overtime pay is usually one-and-a-half times the regular pay.

Companies pay long-haul drivers by the mile. Some companies also pay expenses for long overnight trips. These expenses might include food and hotel rooms. Some truck drivers receive

Local tractor-trailer-truck drivers receive hourly pay.

bonuses for driving into big cities such as New York City or Toronto. Driving in large cities is more challenging. Beginning long-haul drivers can make from $20,000 to $25,000 per year. An average truck driver's salary is $33,000 per year. But some drivers make much more.

Belonging to a union can increase a driver's earnings. A union is a group that seeks fair treatment and better pay for workers.

Owner-operators can earn high yearly incomes. But they have to pay their own expenses. After expenses, these drivers earn an average of between $20,000 and $25,000 per year.

Job Outlook

The outlook for tractor-trailer-truck drivers is stable. The field depends upon the economy. A better economy means more jobs for truck drivers. Companies hire more drivers when the amount of goods they have to ship increases.

Belonging to a union can increase a driver's earnings.

PENNSYLVANIA CONFERENCE OF
TEAMSTERS

PHILA., PA.

Chapter 5

Where the Job Can Lead

Some truck driving jobs are physically hard work. The jobs may require heavy lifting or working long hours. Some tractor-trailer-truck drivers move into jobs that do not require driving or lifting.

Related Jobs

Some truck drivers become dispatchers. Dispatchers assign routes to drivers. They also keep track of company trucks.

Dispatchers assign routes to drivers.

Some truck drivers become owner-operators. Owner-operators can work for many different trucking companies. They lend their trucks and services to companies.

Tractor-trailer-truck drivers also may become company managers or safety supervisors. Some may even teach truck driving classes.

The Future

There will always be a need for truck drivers. The need for truck drivers depends on businesses' success. There are many jobs for truck drivers when businesses are doing well. More than three million truck drivers deliver goods every year in the United States.

As many as 450,000 new jobs open for truck drivers each year. Trucking is one of the fastest growing ways of moving goods from one place to another.

More than three million truck drivers deliver goods in the United States every year.

Words to Know

certify (SUR-tuh-fy)—to officially approve
dispatcher (diss-PACH-ur)—a person who assigns routes to drivers and keeps track of company trucks
double (DUH-buhl)—a tractor that pulls two trailers
endorsement (in-DORS-ment)—proof of additional driving abilities
hazardous materials (HAZ-ard-us muh-TIHR-ee-uhlz)—chemicals that could hurt people or make them sick
interstate (IN-tur-state)—across state lines
route (ROUT)—the plan a driver follows while making deliveries
union (YOON-yuhn)—a group that seeks fair treatment and better pay for workers

To Learn More

McGlothlin, Bruce. *Choosing a Career in Transportation.* New York: Rosen Pub. Group, 1996.

Russell, William. *Truckers.* Vero Beach, Fla.: Rourke Press, 1994.

Scharnberg, Ken. *Oportunities in Trucking.* Lincolnwood, Ill.: VGM Career Books, 1992.

Schleifer, Jay. *Big Rigs.* Rollin'. Mankato, Minn.: Capstone Press, 1996.

Useful Addresses

American Trucking Association
Office of Public Affairs
2200 Mill Road
Alexandria, VA 22314

**Professional Truck Drivers Institute
  of America**
8788 Elk Grove Boulevard
Suite 20
Elk Grove, CA 95624

Ontario Trucking Association
555 Dixon Road
Etobicoke, Ontario
M9W 1H8 Canada

Internet Sites

American Trucking Associations
http://www.trucking.org/infocenter/index.html

Motor Vehicle and Transit Drivers
http://www.hrdc-drhc.gc.ca/JobFutures/
    english/volume1/741/741.htm

The Ontario Trucking Association
http://www.ontruck.org

Truckdrivers
http://stats.bls.gov/oco/ocos246.htm

Index